How To Communicate With The One You Love

A Spiritual Communication Guide To Loving Bliss

Dineice Robinson

authorHOUSE®

AuthorHouse™
1663 Liberty Drive, Suite 200
Bloomington, IN 47403
www.authorhouse.com
Phone: 1-800-839-8640

First published by AuthorHouse 11/26/2007

ISBN: 978-1-4343-3051-2 (sc)

Printed in the United States of America
Bloomington, Indiana

This book is printed on acid-free paper.

Special Dedication

Before you enter into this journey, here is a special "Spiritual Note:" <u>Communication is the key factor to building a loving relationship!</u>

Table of Contents

Communication Between One Another

Case Scenario:

He comes home tired from work. We understand that he has worked a stressful eight hour work schedule. He plops his bag in the center of the floor and he throws his jacket across the chair as he flops across the sofa. He calls out for you. "Hey baby can you get me a beer." Whoops maybe a glass of kool-aid; after all this is a Spiritual Christian book. Anyway what type of responder would you most likely be?

   a. Wife - Natural responder (Negative) – "What do you think you're doing just throwing your stuff around after I've been home cleaning and cooking all day. Get your own kool-aid and pick your stuff up off the floor and off the chair."

   b. Husband – Natural responder (Negative) –

"Listen I just came home from a hard day at work and I don't need to be told what to do in "My" own house."

We really know it's God's house for we brought nothing into this world as we will take nothing out of this world - so for those of you who always say "My House" replace it with "God's House" for God gave us the things of the world to produce wealth not us (Deuteronomy 8:18).

Now that we're clear on whose house it truly is, try the "Spiritual" responses to the case scenario above:

c. Wife - Spiritual responder (Loving) - "Honey I've been working really hard around the house today and it would be wonderful if you could get us both some kool-aid while I put your jacket and your bag away."

d. Husband – Spiritual responder (Loving) – "I'm sorry baby I can put them away."

Many of you are probably saying "You wish!" There will be spiritual kindness you'll have to respond with in your relationship (even when you don't want to) in order to set a spiritual foundation for your loved one to follow; a peaceful response shall receive a peaceful reply back and a harsh response shall receive a harsh reply back.

What type of responder are you - Peaceful or Harsh?

Most of the times our natural way of responding will usually reflect the "Negative" response. If we immerse ourselves into following the spiritual way in Christ then our relationship with our loved one will become more like the love of Christ and would reflect a more loving relationship (Ephesians 5:1-2). This is not an easy task but constant spiritual practice will gradually get you to respond in a loving way with peace and calm.

Alright here is an ear opener. Let's switch gears. Come on gentleman how did you really respond.

Take a test:

He's watching the sports channel, okay the NBA finals; forget it – he's watching the Super bowl game. The lovely wife interrupts his game because she needs his help in the kitchen or help with the kids, or she just wants his attention during the time he's watching the game. She says, "Honey I need your help."

The response:

> a. Husband – Natural responder (Negative) – I'm watching the game; can you wait a minute (we know that minute will never come)?"
>
> b. Wife – Natural responder (Negative) - "Look you need to get your priorities straight, I need your help now. What's more important me or the game?" (now that's a question to stay away from ladies, as you know that you are important, but why compete against "Sports").

Here, let's take a different response route:

> c. Husband – Spiritual responder (Loving) - "Hey I'll be right there honey let me put my program on pause."
>
> d. Wife – Spiritual responder (Loving) – "Okay honey."

Alright, everyone should have Tivo or the Dish network by now. With Tivo or the Dish network you can pause a program and avoid all conflict if someone interrupts your show.

If you don't have Tivo or the Dish network you may not want to interrupt a man while watching his sports program, especially the Super bowl. That's just one we must stay away from ladies because don't interrupt me when I'm shopping. Okay have fun laughing at that one. Sorry I couldn't help, but there are some things best left alone and that's "A man sports program" and "A woman shopping" or you can find yourself in Divorce Court. See - this is when you're suppose to laugh! We forget to laugh a little bit when things don't go our way.

Communication begins with how we use our voice. Take a test:

a. Do you raise your voice when you are in disagreement with your spouse?
b. Do you begin every disagreement with "I" (it's all about you)?
c. Do you speak words to break each other down (degrading ones abilities with negative comments)?

If you answered yes to any one of the above questions then you are starting a war. A hot-tempered person stirs up wrath but a patient person calms a quarrel (Proverbs 15:18). Are you hot-tempered or patient? Become calm in all that you say to one another!

Become a Christ-like Communicator when using your voice in disagreement.

Try this:

    a. Be soft spoken when you are in disagreement with your spouse (Proverbs 15:1).
    b. Begin every disagreement with "We" (you are now one, it's not all about you) (Ephesians 5:31).
    c. Speak words to build each other up not tear each other down (Ephesians 4:29).

It is always easy to find fault in each other and discuss the negative things about one another, as that is usually our "Natural" way of responding when things seem to be falling apart in our relationship. Do not judge the other but make corrections in yourself (Luke 6:37 & 41-42).

We must begin to train our minds to respond in the spirit, to speak the good that is in one another, as this form of communication will improve and compliment any negative attributes one may have. Many (marital) relationships suffer hardship because of the negative words that one may speak into existence about the other. Do you know that life and death is in the power of the tongue and what you speak will come to pass (Proverbs 18:21). Do you speak negative about the one you love?

Take a test:

When disagreement occurs in your relationship do you engage in negative name calling against your loved one. We know the harsh reality of anyone ever using negative words against their loved one is discomforting, but our natural mind is guilty of reacting in anger when things don't go our way. Do you call your loved one a negative (bad) name when things don't go your way? If so, then you are responding in anger and you are not of the spirit of Christ-likeness, for He is of Love not of anger.

If you speak negative about the one you love then they can reflect the negative things you say and your relationship will be destroyed by the works of the devil whom you've invited in with your evil words of destruction.

Speak great things about your loved one and watch great things manifest before you. Learn to tell your loved one that they are remarkable, that they are amazing, and that they are astounding aside from any bad attributes that they may possess, and watch the good that you have spoken about them come into existence.

If you are guilty of speaking negative things about your loved one then it is time for you to switch gears and be challenged to speak something good about the one you love and watch them flourish!

Many relationships begin without trust and over time some relationships become untrustworthy:

Try this case scenario:

> a. Your spouse has returned home after being out all night or being out all day and upon their entry into the house you ask "Where have you been?"

We know that communication is absent from a relationship if such an event takes place and such a question must be asked, but let's tackle it anyway because we want to give spiritual guidance.

Let's be honest - there is rarely an acceptable answer to such a question unless the answer is that one has been in a serious accident and was critically injured, but how can that be if they have returned home! A truthful witness does not deceive, but a false witness pours out lies (Proverbs 14:5).

Here is how to deal with a suspicion of the mind: Too often our natural response is to vent our anger, hurt and pain against the one we ought to love, even in their wrong doing. When you argue against your loved one in anger it is the presence of the devil you're really fighting against. As natural beings we must learn to protect ourselves against the wiles of the devil and build up our spirits to know how to identify the devil's attack in our relationship. Begin not to see the flesh before you, which is the face of your loved one, but "rebuke" the presence of the devil's attack in your relationship and he will flee (James 4:7). For it is not mankind we wrestle against but it is the attack of the devil that we must fight against (Ephesians 6:12).

How to protect yourself spiritually from deceitfulness:

Put on the full armor of God, build up your spirit, emulate Godly behavior, cease from anger and forsake wrath; do not fret---it only causes harm (Psalm 37:8) and "you" ill health. Stay humble in your spirit and don't allow the devil to take your spirit from you with his ways of deceit, which will remove you from the love of God and God's blessings for your life (Romans 8:35-39).

Be not concerned about the deceitful ways of another and let not your heart be troubled but believe that God is your stronghold in the day of trouble (John 14:1 & Nahum 1:7). Let your spirit remove you peacefully from situations that will cause you suspicion of the mind and unrest "Not Your Anger." So if you feel the ways of deceit is consuming your relationship remove yourself spiritually with Love. All things can be settled peacefully if you build up your spirit against the attacks of the devil. For what's done in the dark will soon come into the light and Satan will be crushed under your feet shortly (Romans 16:20). Remove yourself peacefully.

There will be times when you want to walk away from imitating the Love of God in your relationship but you'll only be destroying your own soul; for the loving ways of the Lord are always right (Proverbs 10:7-14).

Let me share a case scenario with you.

Case Scenario:

Have you ever forgotten about a very special day that was important in your relationship; like your Anniversary, your loved one's Birthday, Mother's day for your loved one, Father's day for your loved one, or maybe you didn't forget about the special day but you had no desire to make a big celebration out of it.

Response:

    a.   Honey, I bought you flowers and a card for our Anniversary to celebrate the years we've been together, and the only thing you did was said "Happy Anniversary!" I mean, you didn't buy me anything.

Although it is important to acknowledge special dates in your relationship, too many times when we "Give" we often expect something in return. Do not look for returns on your givings from someone you love but give from your heart. Love must be "Unconditional," not with "Conditions." It is important that we show love through our actions not our pocket book, for those things can perish. Don't be angered by putting a value on your relationship. Allow their actions to show that they care.

Actions that show one care – take a test.

a. Do you show one another love each day (1st John 4:7-21)?
b. Do you speak words of kindness that constantly build each other up (Ephesians 4:29)?

If you answered "yes" to the above questions then you are a true example of showing actions like the love of Christ. If you answered "no" to the above questions then you have some work to do!

Celebrate the special dates in your relationship with unconditional love; not with love that has conditions! "Acknowledge and Remember" the special dates!

I often hear that old cliché that "You pick your own battles" and I often wonder why we battle at all, but here's one to stay away from:

Are you guilty of this case scenario:

You're sitting in the passenger seat of the car and your loved one is driving. You the passenger, who now wants to become the driver from the passenger seat, begins to say to your loved one "Speed up" because their driving too slow or to "Slow down" because their driving too fast or "Watch that hole up ahead," or you simply direct them to drive faster so that they can make the next traffic light. Annoying yet? Do you often wonder why the passenger just didn't do the driving, seems they know more!

The Responder (Driver):

   a. Natural Responder (Negative) – Would you let me drive or I can pull over and you can drive.

   b. Spiritual Responder (Loving) – Honey I appreciate your help but relax - you're safe with me.

The "Spirit" has an awesome loving response, so much more different than the "Natural" negative response! Which response above do you believe would bring peace? Which responder would you want in your relationship? If you selected "b," the Spiritual Responder, then peace will be brought into your relationship. We all must be accountable for how we respond even when annoyed. To receive peace in your relationship begin to emulate a spiritual response like Christ.

Many challenges will come before you in your relationship when responding to one another, and it will not always be easy to go "Spiritual," but that is why it is important to begin establishing a spiritual baseline early on in your relationship as this will bring about constant spiritual bliss in your relationship. The challenge is to speak slowly so that you can hear your spiritual response before you react quickly to your natural way of responding (retaliation) when in disagreement.

Did you know that "Facial Expressions" can often speak louder than words? Are you guilty of showing negative facial expressions of disgust and frustration towards your loved one when differences occur? If your facial expression appears to show disgust and frustration when in discussion with the one you love then you have already allowed a negative presence of the devil to enter into the room. Don't welcome the expression of the devil to appear into your relationship with negative facial expressions. It is important to allow your facial expression to reflect an expression of spiritual peace and calm, even when in disagreement with your loved one!

I often wonder why couples are so quick to show anger towards each other and present a spiritual kindness around external forces they interact with, such as their Boss, Co-workers, Friends their Pastor etc. Would you ever express anger towards the external forces you interact with the way that you express anger towards the one you promised to love and honor?

Take a test:

Case Scenario 1:

a. Your "Boss" approaches you and informs you that you need to stay late after work to improve your work production to help maintain the company quota.

Case Scenario 2:

b. Your "Loved One" approach you and informs you that they need more help from you with the cooking and cleaning around the house to help maintain a balanced household.

How would you respond to your "Boss" request? How would you respond to your "Loved One" request?

Would you be quick tempered in anger with your loved one and spiritually kind to your boss (the external force)? No matter what the case scenario may be, If you are quick tempered with your loved one and present spiritual kindness to your boss then you have encountered the practice of being a hypocrite in God's sight (Matthew 7:5). Do not pretend to be spiritually grounded (loving and kind) around external forces if you are not spiritually grounded in your relationship with the one you promised love.

There may be many times your loved one may tempt you to want to express anger and frustration through your facial expressions, but show an expression of love at all times to the one you promised to love and honor, and to all those external forces around you. Be "Consistent" in showing love - not a "Hypocrite!"

Who's in control of your tongue? The spirit of God or Satan?

Take a Test:

Do you have a physical beauty on the outside but curse using bad language when in discussion with your loved one? How ones beauty can often deceive others! Allow your physical beauty on the outside to be a reflection of what comes out of your mouth! Have you ever wondered how one can have such a physical beauty but yet speak with evil profanity.

The cursing of the tongue has become the most powerful weapon that destroys relationships. Have you struggled with the tongue during discussions in your relationship? Are you guilty of the curse?

If you answered "yes" then your demonic ways of the tongue will destroy God's will for your life, your soul and your relationship. As we are all created from the image of God we know that God is not of evil speaking. If you are one to use profanity when communicating with your loved one then you have allowed the works of the devil to "control" you and your relationship and set a snare for your own soul (James 4:11-12). The devil comes to kill, steal and destroy if you allow him any space into the temple of God, which is your body (1st Corinthians 6:19). Do not allow the devil to speak through you with the cursing of the tongue and destroy the temple of God or it will be the destruction of your relationship and your own soul (John 10:10).

Seek the spirit of God and stop the cursing so that your physical beauty can be the reflection of what comes out of your mouth! Is your relationship headed towards destruction? If yes, then check the cursing of the tongue!

Have you been living in your comfort zone? Are you a sweet loving person to your loved one when things are comfortable to you? How do you respond when circumstances in your relationship makes you uncomfortable? Do you respond with anger or with spiritual love?

Take a test:

If you come home from work and the house is not clean or dinner is not on the table are you rude and unpleasantly loud to your loved one when circumstances removes you out of your comfort zone?

If you answered "yes" then you are living in your comfort zone. Don't let an uncomfortable interruption in your day drive you to anger against the one you promised love and honor! Remove yourself from your comfort zone and prepare for "Uncomfortable" circumstances with love, and not anger. It is important to build up your spirit to be loving and remain respectful to one another even when things become uncomfortable in your relationship!

Transform your spirit to respond in love even when it pushes you outside of your comfort zone, and you shall flourish through God's sight (Psalm 92:12-13)!

Communication About Kids

Here is a thought; communicating about kids (this may be your biggest challenge). Do not let kids be the ruin of a wonderful union between two people, but learn how to respond with compassion when communicating about kids. Kids often become the biggest discussion in relationships. There was an old cliché that "Kids Will Make Or Break A Marriage," something I have grown not to believe. It is the natural "negative" response and actions of adults, during communication about kids that will make or break a marriage.

Is your marriage breaking up over the discussion about kids?

Try this:

You come home from work and enter the house and toys are covering the floor. How do you respond:

a. Natural Responder (Negative) – "Honey I can never get in the house because the kids toys are spreaded across the floor. Can you make the kids pick up their toys or will you clean up behind them so I can relax when I come home. I mean, you're home all day!"

How would you respond back? Should you lash out at your loved one and begin explaining all that you have done for the day (this is where the battle begins) or will you take the "Spiritual" way out and respond with a gentle answer – (Proverbs 15:1-2) – what a challenge to be like Christ! It takes a person who love and fear God to respond with a gentle answer. Who do you love and fear most, God or mankind? If you love and fear God more than mankind then keep peace in your spirit, don't let the devil stir you up and remove you from the love of God but respond back with a gentle answer.

Negative responders; do not be quickly provoked in your spirit, for anger resides in the lap of fools (Ecclesiastes 7:9). Be patient, for one that controls their temper can receive a lifetime of favor from the Lord (Proverbs 16:32 – Psalms 37:27). Do not hinder your own blessings and give in to negative speaking. Don't be a fool!

Here's another case scenario:

The lovely wife has been home all day changing diapers, washing clothes, preparing dinner and helping the kids with homework. We all know that this is an enormous task and usually takes up an entire 24 hour day (most of us would rather work an 8 hour job outside of the home; at least you get a lunch and two breaks). Your wonderful husband comes home after working a regular stressful 8 hour workday and you want a break now from the rigorous duties of being the housewife and caregiver to the kids. What do you say to him when he enters the house?

  a. Wife -Natural responder (Negative) – "I'm glad you're home, now you can get the kids so I can get a break. Here's the bottle for lil Brandon, and Johnny needs a bath, I'm going out for a while."

  b. Husband – Natural responder (Negative) – "Well wait a minute, where are you going? I worked all day and I need a break to; I can't do all this while you're gone - you just can't leave."

See this is great! You're tired and he's tired and no one wants to be with the kids now—this is where the battle begins. Be a fly on the wall in this house. Do you ever greet your spouse by just saying "Hello honey how was your day" before you begin addressing all the problems of the day?

Try this response:

    c. Wife – Spiritual responder (Loving) – "Hi honey how was your day? You must be tired, let me get you something to drink (kool-aid, not beer we're still in the Spirit). I've prepared your dinner and it's on the stove. I'll need for you to watch the kids after you eat so I can go out to the gym and take a break from the kids."

    d. Husband - Spiritual responder (Loving) – "That's fine honey. Let me just get myself situated and you can take off."

I know you're asking yourself "Who would ever communicate with such consideration and respect?" I can tell you that "spiritual" people would communicate so respectfully and considerably because people living in the "natural" will curse you out! Is there spiritual love in your relationship or will you curse them out?

Changing the way we communicate with one another about kids, under stressful moments, will determine whether your relationship is pleasant or unpleasant. Be considerate and sensitive to one another. Begin to speak slowly but listen carefully (James 1:19-20). You will begin to thank God for silencing you so that you can hear your spirit respond in a loving way.

Of course it takes two people to work at this, but since you can only change yourself, then your own spiritual connection to change yourself will soon become a reflection for those around you to begin to emulate a loving spirit also because you have set a spiritual foundation of peace in the way you respond. So don't be overcome by evil but overcome evil with good (Romans 12:21). Begin the process – Take The Challenge to become more like Christ in your (marital) relationship!

Communication About
Family Members

Have you ever been compared to a family member? I'm sure we all have been compared to some family member in our extended family by our spouse. The comparison is generally about whom we look like or who we act like, but not every comparison is complimentary.

Case Scenario:

Your spouse tells you that you act just like your mother or father and that you are very selfish or stubborn. How would you really respond to that - "Naturally" or "Spiritually?"

Here is the dilemma – not only is your "natural" way of responding is to defend yourself but now you "naturally" feel that it is your responsibility to also defend a loving parent (what a double battle). Now this is where the devil can begin to devour your relationship if you don't do good for the evil comparison that is made about you. How can you respond in a "spiritual" loving way to ease the "natural" anger you are feeling from what was just said about you so negatively. One should never compare a spouse to a family member in a negative way, especially targeting parents, as this is quite rude; for love does not behave rudely (1st Corinthians 13:5). This is an attack of the devil. So do not avenge yourself, and give in to the wrath, for Vengeance is the Lord's and He will repay the wrongdoer (Romans 12:19). It is said that a wise person will depart from evil, but a fool rages and acts in foolish ways and is not careful (Proverbs 14:16-17).

Take a test:

Would you respond "Naturally" like a raging fool that is not careful or will you respond "Spiritually" and be wise and walk away and let Vengeance be the Lord? What type of responder are you?

Know that you can do all things through Christ who strengthens you (Philippians 4:13). Become silent and walk away or have a soft answer; for a harsh word will stir up anger and you shall be in danger of judgment for yourself (Proverbs 15:1 & Matthew 5:22-23). If you fear God then place no judgment upon yourself being vengeful and stay in God's presence with kindness. For those who see the presence of your spiritual reaction will soon follow your imitation of Christ-likeness or soon they will flee like the devil.

There will be many times we'll have to wrestle with our "Natural" response in order to respond in the "Spirit." Challenge yourself to become a "Spiritual" responder in your relationship. Blessed are those who maintain justice, who constantly do what is right (Psalm 106:3).

Extended family will be one of many encounters that will be discussed in relationships, such as who family will be visited during the holidays when there are different geographical locations involved. We must learn to respond with spiritual guidelines when communicating matters that may cause disagreement. It will be important to remain silent and listen to your spirit when things don't go your way and refrain from reacting naturally with anger. Many of our muscles contract and tense up when we feel threaten and the need to become defensive. Let your spirit calm your muscles to respond gently and without hatred. Be obedient to the Lord and do what is right and good in the Lord's sight so that you may receive the blessings the Lord has promised (Deuteronomy 30:15-16).

I know most of you would rather respond back naturally because it often feels satisfying to strike back against someone who has hurt you so badly, especially a loved one; but continue to ask yourself "Who do you love and fear most," the Lord or mankind? If you love and fear the Lord more than mankind then follow the Lord's commandment that no one renders evil for evil to anyone, but always pursue what is good for yourself and for all (1st Thessalonians 5:15).

We must begin to fear the Lord more and stay in his presence with goodness so that your day of judgment will be pleasing to the Lord and not destroyed by the evil works of the devil.

Communication
About Friends

As a marriage is formed between two people, friends are usually transferred over into the union and not all friends are received or accepted by the other spouse. Many couples struggle with being married to a spouse who may have many single friends that they continuously spend time with throughout the marriage.

Case Scenario:

Your spouse spends more time with their friends than with you.

Too often we fail to communicate in a spiritual realm about the concerns in our relationship.

Take a test:

If your spouse spends more time with their friends than with you – how would you address the issue?

a. Natural response (negative) – "You're spending an awful lot of time with your friends; have you forgotten that you married me not your friends?"

b. Spiritual response (loving) – "It would be wonderful if we could spend more time together because I miss you when you're not here with me."

Which response do you think would invite the devil into your relationship? A

Which response do you think would invite the Love of Christ into your relationship? B

Who do you want to invite into your relationship? Invite the love of Christ into your relationship – for he who is slow to get angry has great understanding (Proverbs 14:29).

It can be difficult to change our way of communicating to become spiritual if we have been reacting to our natural feelings over time. Allow your relationship to become wholesome in love and seek the knowledge of Christ in your response.

If you have been spending more time with your friends than with the one you promised to love, then it is time for you to put on the new man and follow the blue print of the one that created you. When you have great understanding of God you will be able to say "NO" to the things (friends) that may separate you from the one you promised to love (2nd Peter 1:6). Spend time with each other responding in love so that your relationship can be filled with loving bliss.

Many couples struggle with a spouse who may have too many single friends of the opposite sex whom they continuously spend time with. Do not indulge yourself in the sinful things of the world which can come from the wrong desires of your flesh – gain the knowledge of self-control (2nd Peter 4-5). Be continuously fulfilled with one another in joy, peace and comfort or the devil will tempt you to do those things which you know you should not do. Follow God's will for your marriage. Marriage should be respected by everyone for God will punish those who are not faithful in marriage (Hebrews 13:4). Don't allow time spent with those of the opposite sex lead you to do wrong by your own temptation as the sin of the wrong you do will bring death and destruction in your life(James 1:15).

Don't let friends (even those of the opposite sex) destroy your relationship. Friends may come and go but if you put "God's" love in your marriage it will last forever!

Communication About Blended Families

Many times the union between a couple that brings kids into the household from another relationship (Blended Family) can be most challenging if we are not careful in how we communicate.

Would you respond "Naturally (negative) or Spiritually (loving)" to the case scenarios below while in the presence of your child and your spouse, who is Step-parent ?

Case Scenarios:

> a. Your child confronts you and begins to tell you about the extreme amount of chores that has been assigned to them by the step-parent.

b. Your adult child wants to move back into the house with you and the Step-parent.

c. Your child confronts you about the rules and the discipline imposed on them by the Step-parent.

There are many situations that can occur with blended family matters that may bring about challenges. How one communicates will be the determining factor for establishing the foundation for the relationship. If using the "natural" response for any case scenario above you will be quick to speak and slow to listen without much thought about what to say (this can stir up strife). A "spiritual" response will be slow to speak and will listen with much love (this will bring peace).

What type of responder would you be?

Many times with blended families the biological parent will find themselves in a dilemma to choose between their child and their spouse, which can cause the destruction of the union if spiritual practices and actions are absent from the relationship. In many sensitive situations pertaining to kids it becomes a challenge for adults to refrain from discussing conflicting matters (about the child) in the presence of the child.

There are times when parenting adults will find themselves in the presence of the child when conflicting matters occur. It is important to "AVOID" discussing conflicting matters in the presence of children for they will learn the ways of conflict and be in danger of setting a snarl for their own souls (Proverbs 22:24-25). Do not expose children into the midst of confusion. Develop spiritually to work hard to live together in peace and with kindness (Ephesians 4:2-3).

Bottom Line: The way you respond ("Naturally or Spiritually") will be the determining factor in blended family ties or destruction.

Communication About Finances

Now who does not like money! We've heard that old cliché that "Money is the root of all evil (Hebrews 13:5)." Whoever trusts in his riches will fall, but the righteous will thrive like a green leaf (Proverbs 11:28). Don't greed over money but use it righteously. Couples will find themselves having many discussions about the finances in their relationship. Many break-ups occur in relationships due to "natural" responses about money.

Do you use any of the following phrases in your relationship?

- "It's my money"
- "I pay for everything"
- "When I get my check"

- "I pay all the bills with my money"
- "I have my own accounts"

If you have used any of the above phrases in your relationship then hear what God has to say to you:

God says whoever loves money never has money enough; whoever loves wealth is never satisfied with his income. A stingy man is eager to get rich and is unaware that poverty awaits him (Ecclesiastes 5:10 & Proverbs 28:22). Don't be eager to separate your finances from what God has made to be a union of "ONE" whom you shall share all things with (Ephesians 5:31).

Are you in a relationship that has already fallen apart but you stay in it for the convenience of the finances. We often find ourselves trapped in a relationship for financial convenience but it can also cause us ill health (Proverbs 14:30).

Don't let financial stability from someone be your power source but seek God as he will be your power source to financial prosperity. He will show his love and kindness, to all that are good, in their time of need (Isaiah 30:19). Lean not on your own natural ability to understand but rest in your spirit that you shall hear a word from God in giving you direction to the riches of His glory (Isaiah 30:21-23). Don't be devoured by ill health by making mankind the power source to your financial stability but dwell in prayer as God will respond to the prayer of those in need; he will not despise their plea (Psalm 102:17) and he can peacefully set you apart from those that greed.

How do you approach your loved one when money matters occur - Naturally or Spiritually?

Take a test.

Case Scenario:

Natural Approach (Negative):

You say to your loved one: "You are spending way too much money on things "You" don't need, "You" need to watch your spending because we can't afford the things "You" are buying."

The "natural" approach above can certainly create conflict and may cause one to become defensive as everything has just been directed against one person by using the word **"<u>YOU</u>."** Marriage is to be holy and without blame (Ephesians 5:27).

Although it may be one spouse causing financial burdens in the relationship, it is important that we "first" learn how to "Address" one another when money matters occur. We all know that money is a very sensitive subject that must be discussed in a relationship, but we must learn to discuss it with grace and compassion exemplifying the love of Christ (Psalm 145:8).

Try this:

Spiritual Approach (Loving):

You say to your loved one: "We need to monitor "Our" spending so that we can eliminate some cost factors that's taking us over "Our" budget. We can begin to save to pay off some debt and take a trip together if we reduce "Our" spending."

With this "spiritual" approach no one person is being blamed, it has become a joint venture by simply saying **"OUR."** Relationships should not be to point blame (which is what the natural response usually does really well) but to address the matters as a union of "One" using words such as "Our or We" not "You or I." You can now begin to peacefully discuss how to eliminate the excessive spending with the spiritual approach used.

Remember that old cliché "It's not what you say but it's how you say it." It really stands true to the Word of God (Proverbs 15:2).

If you are thinking that it would feel too strange to communicate in such a loving way, then you are beginning to understand the spirit. Remember the spirit responds different than the natural and the spiritual response is often seen as strange. Become "strange" begin responding in the spirit.

Naturally we fail to listen to our spirit and put God in our (marital) relationship. This is when relationships begin to tumble and fall apart if a spiritual baseline is not developed and put into practice. If there is anything to learn about achieving loving bliss in your relationship, that is to involve the love of Christ in your relationship and do all things in "LOVE" or your relationship will be devoured by the devil.

Communication Is Absent "Spiritually"

How to tell when "Spiritual" communication is absent from your relationship:

- When you raise your voice in anger.
- When you show facial expressions of frustration and anger.
- When you break each other down with negative speaking.
- When you allow the cursing (profanity) of the devil to speak through you when communicating.

If this is your relationship then spiritual communication is missing and destruction will overcome.

Communication Into Loving Bliss

Here are some words of substitution to say to one another when in disagreement to begin your journey into Loving Bliss.

Spiritual "Loving" Words To Say	Natural "Negative" Words To Stay Away From
It would be wonderful if we……..	You need to………
It would be nice if we……..	You never……..
That made me feel……..	You always make me feel……
"WE" should…….	"YOU" should………

When in disagreement we often point the finger at the other person. Natural "negative" responses are usually words of judgment and condemnation and often begins with the word "You" - for "You" should not judge nor condemn another (Luke 6:37).

Naturally we fail to listen to our spirit and put God in our relationship and then we begin to wonder why things are falling apart.

Have you been breaking down your relationship with words and actions of destruction over time and now you're wondering why it's falling apart. You have invited the curse of Satan into your relationship with words and actions of destruction.

It is too often we spend more time breaking each other down instead of building each other up despite the bad attributes in one another. Do all things according to the Lord's commandments or your relationship will be destroyed by the devil. Involve the love of Christ in your (marital) relationship!

Again, it will be a challenge to be imitators of Christ (Loving) all the time but how do you think Jesus felt! Remember that old cliché "If he (Christ) can do it than I can do it to!" Begin to emulate the love of

Christ in your relationship and fall into Loving Bliss with the one you Love.

"If Jesus could do it than you can do it to!"

Become a new person and develop a spiritual baseline for yourself and grow together in Love (2nd Corinthians 5:17).

Now put on the new you and communicate in the "Spirit!" When you face your "Natural" situations with a "Spiritual" response you'll win all the time (2nd Peter 3:7-10)!

Let the journey into Loving Bliss begin!